GW01459069

Rose

AND
Her Fairy Shoes

Written by

Grace Cotterell-Moore, Illustrated by The Autist

In the forest lived a little fairy, her name was Rose Petal.
She liked to skip along and sing to herself.
The other fairies thought she was a little odd as
she never wore fairy slippers.

Rose was happy by herself, but she longed for someone to play with.

She would sit in a tree and watch as the other fairies played.

2

One day, an owl settled on the branch next to her and asked:

"Why don't you join in with the other fairies?"

3.

"I don't know how," said Rose.
I'm scared that they won't like me.

"Maybe it's because I don't wear fairy slippers."

"Why don't you wear fairy slippers?" asked the owl.

"I don't like the way that they feel on my feet," replied Rose.

The owl thought about how he could help Rose.

4.

Tomorrow
will be
NO
SLIPPERS
DAY

He made a poster and said,
"Attention, All fairies!"

All the fairies came to him and asked how they would walk around the forest without fairy slippers.

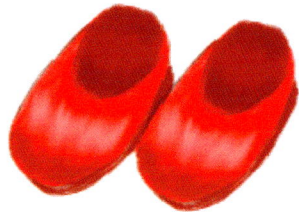

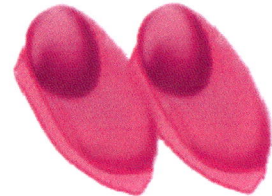

5.

He replied, "Maybe you don't need fairy slippers to walk around. Rose doesn't wear fairy slippers maybe you should ask her."

One by one, the fairies asked Rose if she could help them get around the forest without fairy slippers on their feet.

"Can you help us please?"

"With what?" asked Rose.

"You never wear fairy slippers, how do you get around the forest without hurting your feet?"

"Easy," said Rose, "I make my own shoes."

6.

The fairies gasped –

"You don't buy shoes from
the fairy slipper shop?!"

Fairy
Slippers

7.

"No," said Rose, "It's much more fun
to make my own." "But how?" asked
the fairies. "I'll show you," said Rose.

Rose explained, "You can make anything fit your feet, if you know how, it doesn't have to be fairy slippers."

"Like what?" asked the fairies.

"Tree Bark, flower Petals, Mushrooms, anything."

"You could use berries like Raspberries and Blackberries."

9

"Pine cones are sturdy and hollowed out, they look great."

"Blueberries are great for dyeing things."

"Tree sap can be used to stick things together."

"Small twigs, branches, and tree twine can be used to tie the shoe materials together."

10.

All the other forest fairies gathered together lots of different forest things to make their shoes, but they didn't know where to start.

11.

"We should ask Rose for help!" Rose was a little worried when she saw all the fairies coming towards her.

"Please, Rose, will you help us?"
"Of course," replied Rose.

She gathered all the fairies in a circle with
all the bits and bobs they had collected.

Rose asked each fairy to choose an item, then she showed
them how to make each one into a pair of shoes.

Rose was so happy to see all of the fairies
working together and having a good time.

She was also busy going around each fairy
and helping to make their shoes.

"See! Shoes that aren't slippers!"

All the fairies danced in their new shoes,
each one unique to them.

14

"Which shoes do you like the most?"
a fairy asked Rose.

Rose smiled.

The fairies were interested in what she had to say!

"My leaf shoes are the best, they are so comfy to dance in, and I can tie them with lots of different things. You can even match them with your outfits!" she said.

The fairies thought that Rose was so clever!
They asked her if they could do the fairy dance with her
on No Slippers Day!

17

"Yes!" said Rose. "I would really like that!"

Rose was so grateful to the Wise Old
Owl for coming up with No Slippers Day.

"Thank you!" she said, visiting him in his tree house.

"You're very welcome, Rose. Everyone loves your shoes!" he replied.

18

19

She was so excited to see every fairy at the celebration later that evening and even more excited to see their beautiful fairy shoes.

They danced all night long under the stars,
and not once did their feet hurt!

20

Rose's shoes were so popular that the fairies wanted her to help them make more shoes with different designs and different materials.

Every day, the fairies would see Rose dancing and singing, and they would all put on their handmade shoes and sing and dance around the forest with her.

22

from then on, Rose was included in every celebration with the other fairies.

Rose was so happy, she had friends to play with, and they didn't care that she didn't wear fairy slippers.

She was not odd, she was
Rose Petal Leaf

23

24